Novels for Students, Volume 2

Copyright © 1997
Gale Research
835 Penobscot Building
645 Griswold St.
Detroit, Ml 48226-4094

This book is printed on acid-free paper that meets the minimum requirements of American National Standard for Information Sciences—Permanence Paper for Printed Library Materials, ANSI Z39.48-1984.

ISBN 0-7876-1687-7
ISSN 1094-3552

Printed in the United States of America
10 9 8 7 6 5 4

A Separate Peace

John Knowles 1959

Introduction

Since it was first published in 1959, John Knowles's novel *A Separate Peace* has gradually acquired the status of a minor classic. Set in the summer of 1942 at a boys' boarding school in New Hampshire, the novel focuses on the relationship between two roommates and best friends, Gene Forrester and Phineas. Both approaching their last year of high school and anticipating their involvement in World War II, Gene and Phineas have very different dispositions. Gene, from whose point of view *A Separate Peace* is told, is a somewhat athletic, shy intellectual; Phineas is a reckless non-intellectual and the best athlete at the school. As an adult looking back fifteen years, Gene recalls and comes to terms with an act he committed that left his friend physically incapacitated and ultimately contributed to his death. While daring each other to jump from a tree in a cold river, Gene jounces the limb Phineas is standing on. The latter lands on the bank of river, shattering several bones and terminating his athletic career.

A Separate Peace, which evolved from Knowles's short story "Phineas," brought its author both critical and commercial success. First published in England, it received excellent reviews there. Many critics praised the novel for its rich characterizations, artful symbolism, and effective narrative. Despite its success in England, eleven publishers in the United States turned it down before Macmillan decided to publish the American edition. As in England, the novel received excellent notices in the U.S. press. Many critics noted that the novel could be read as an allegory about the causes of war. Although *A Separate Peace* did not become an instant best-seller——only selling seven thousand copies in its first American printing—it has gradually become a commercial success, selling more than nine million copies to date.

Author Biography

John Knowles was born on 16 September 1926, in the coal mining town of Fairmont, West Virginia. He was the third child of James Myron and Mary Beatrice Shea Knowles. At the age of fifteen, Knowles attended New Hampshire's prestigious Phillips Exeter Academy. The Devon School, where most of the action of A *Separate Peace* takes place, is based on Phillips Exeter, and many of Knowles' friends and acquaintances at Phillips Exeter were incorporated into the novel. In a *New York Times* interview, Knowles confirmed that the novel's "Super Suicide Society," in which members jumped from a tree into the river, really did exist at Exeter. Although not rendered permanently physically handicapped like Phineas, Knowles, after an unfortunate leap, spent most of the summer of 1943 on crutches.

After graduation from Exeter, Knowles entered Yale University for the 1944 fall term before going into the U.S. Army Air Force. Following his discharge from the service in November 1945, he reentered Yale. As a college student, Knowles submitted stories to the *Yale Record*, the college humor magazine. In 1949, he graduated with a B.A. in English; from 1950 to 1952, he worked as a drama critic and reporter for the *Hartford Courant* in Hartford, Connecticut. In the early 1950s, his novel *Descent to Proselito* was accepted for publication, but Knowles withdrew it on the advice of his mentor, the famous writer Thornton Wilder. In 1953, *Story Magazine* published his first story, "A Turn in the Sun." In 1956, *Cosmopolitan* published Knowles's short story "Phineas," which was later expanded into A *Separate Peace.*

By the middle 1950s, Knowles had become a member of the editorial staff of *Holiday* and was living in Philadelphia. He was also starting work on the novel that would become his most famous work: *A Separate Peace.*

In an *Esquire* article from 1985 entitled "My Separate Peace," Knowles recalled that writing the manuscript for *A Separate Peace* came quickly and easily for him. Working on a regular schedule, Knowles usually went to bed at midnight, awoke at seven, wrote for an hour, turning out five to six hundred words, then went to his job at *Holiday.* He believed "No book can have been easier to get down on paper," adding, "... A *Separate Peace* wrote itself." Getting the book published, however, did not come easily at all. Turning the manuscript over to a literary agent, Knowles saw his book rejected by eleven publishers. Knowles recalled the most common reaction was "Who's going to want to read about a bunch of prep boys and what happened to them long ago in the past?" Finally, in 1959, the London publisher Secker and Warburg agreed to put out the British edition of the novel. After the book opened to almost unanimous praise from English reviewers, Macmillan brought out the American edition in 1960. A *Separate Peace* did equally well in the United States with the American critics. With the stunning success of the novel, Knowles quit his job at *Holiday* and was able to devote himself to writing fiction—a luxury that very few American writers had then or have today.

Following A *Separate Peace*, Knowles went on to publish several other novels, including *Morning in Antibes* (1962), *Indian Summer* (1966), *The Paragon* (1971), *Spreading Fires*, and A *Vein of Riches* (1974). In 1981, he published *Peace Breaks Out*—the sequel to *A Separate Peace*—which retained the Devon School setting but had a different cast of characters. While *Peace Breaks Out* did not receive as favorable reviews as *A Separate Peace*, some critics commended the sequel for solid characterization and tight plotting.

Plot Summary

In John Knowles's *A Separate Peace*, Gene Forrester returns to visit New Hampshire's Devon School after a fifteen-year absence. He recalls his complex relationship with his roommate and best friend Phineas. His narrative begins during the summer of 1942, when Phineas goads him into jumping off a tree into the Devon River. Phineas—nicknamed Finny—is the best athlete in school, with a charismatic personality that wins over both teachers and students. He lives a life ruled by inspiration and anarchy, following his own set of rules and appearing tireless. Gene has mixed feelings about Phineas: despite his admiration and gratitude for their friendship, he envies Finny's apparent ease and the charm which allows him to break school rules without reproof. Nevertheless, when Phineas suggests they form a secret society, whose membership requires jumping from the tree into the river, Gene agrees.

When Gene fails a test after a clandestine trip to the beach with Phineas, he decides that Finny is trying to jeopardize his studies. One night before another exam, Phineas asks Gene to come to the tree to witness Leper Lepellier make the jump. Gene declines, saying that he needs to study. When Phineas accepts his excuse, Gene realizes his suspicions were unfounded. This makes him feel inferior to Phineas. He stops studying, visits the tree, and agrees to Finny's suggestion of jumping from the tree together. When they're both balanced on its branch, Gene jiggles it and Phineas falls to the ground.

Phineas's leg is shattered, and he recovers in the infirmary and later at home in Boston. He doesn't mention Gene's part in the accident, nor does anyone else. During his absence, Gene tries on Finny's clothes and feels like him, which gives him confidence. Dr. Stanpole tells Gene that Phineas will recover, but will never participate in sports again. Gene visits Finny on his way back to school after his vacation, and is shocked to see him looking like an invalid. He decides to tell Phineas the accident was his fault.

> My blood could start to pound if it wanted to; let it. I was going ahead. "I was thinking about you most of the trip up."
>
> "Oh, yeah?" He glanced briefly into my eyes.
>
> "I was thinking about you ... and the accident."
>
> "There's loyalty for you. To think about me when you were on a vacation."
>
> "I was thinking about it ... about you because—I was thinking about you and the accident because I caused it."
>
> Finny looked steadily at me, his face very handsome and expressionless.

"What do you mean, you caused it?" his voice was as steady as his eyes.

My own voice sounded quiet and foreign. "I jounced the limb. I caused it." One more sentence. "I deliberately jounced the limb so you would fall off."

He looked older than I had ever seen him. "Of course you didn't."

"Yes I did. I did!"

"Of course you didn't do it. You damn fool. Sit down, you damn fool."

"Of course I did!"

"I'm going to hit you if you don't sit down."

"Hit me!" I looked at him. *"Hit* me!" You can't even get up! You can't even come near me!"

Phineas ends their discussion by telling Gene he's tired and Gene leaves, deciding to make things up to Finny once he's back at school.

Phineas telephones Gene at school. Upon learning that Gene doesn't have another roommate, he's reassured that Gene didn't mean what he said about the accident. He refuses to accept Gene's decision to become Assistant Senior Crew manager, commenting: "Listen, pal, if I can't play sports, *you're* going to play them for me." His words help

Gene realize that one of his purposes was to become a part of Phineas. When Brinker Hadley, the head student, heckles Gene about the accident, Gene ignores the teasing although he feels terribly guilty. One afternoon, Brinker and Gene meet Leper, whose nonsensical comments drive Brinker to decide to enlist in the army. Gene is tempted to do the same. He regards enlisting as a way of escaping the past and entering adulthood. Feeling that he owes nothing to anyone, except himself, he returns to his room to find Phineas, who has returned to school.

The next morning, Brinker asks Gene about enlisting with him. Gene realizes that Phineas needs him and changes his mind. Phineas announces his intention to groom Gene for the 1944 Olympics, in which he had intended to participate before the accident. Gene begins tutoring Finny in academics and Finny tutors Gene in athletics. When a teacher declares that the purpose of exercise is to prepare for war, Phineas reminds Gene of his theory that the war is really a conspiracy amongst the world's leaders. He states his theory so convincingly that Gene momentarily believes him. Nevertheless, when Leper enlists after seeing a propaganda film, Gene joins the others in creating an heroic fantasy life for Leper. Brinker drops his enlistment plan after Gene decides not to join him and becomes a quiet rebel, quitting most of the school activities in which he's been involved.

Phineas suggests holding a winter carnival. Once the games begin, he performs a dance of joy on the prize table. Gene becomes the star of Phineas's gala and surpasses himself, feeling liberated during "this afternoon of momentary, illusory, special and separate peace." The festivities end when a cryptic telegram from Leper arrives, saying that he's escaped and needs help. Gene travels to Leper's home in Vermont, where he discovers that Leper has deserted and is suffering mental problems. Leper calls Gene a savage underneath, taunting him for having knocked Phineas out of the tree. Gene returns to school, desperate to see Phineas, and finds him in the middle of a snowball fight. Gene joins in and enjoys the fight's vitality and energy, though he wonders what will happen when they all get drafted. When Brinker asks Gene about Leper, he admits that Leper has cracked up. Brinker observes that two of their classmates—Leper and Phineas—have already been sidelined from the war. Brinker confronts Gene, insisting that they have to stop pitying Phineas so that life can go on. Phineas tells Gene he's changed his mind about the war, because he saw Leper outside the school and believes that the war caused his breakdown.

That night, Brinker takes Gene and Phineas to the Assembly Room for a mock inquiry about Finny's accident. Phineas remembers climbing the tree and falling out, and asks Gene whether he noticed the tree shaking. Gene says he doesn't recall anything like that. Phineas then remembers his suggestion they make a double jump, and that they started to climb. Someone else says Leper was there, and he's brought in. Leper admits that he saw

Gene and Phineas on the tree limb, adding that they moved up and down like a piston. When Brinker insists upon getting all the facts, Phineas loses control, rushes from the Assembly Room, and falls down the marble stairs, breaking his leg again.

Dr. Stanpole comments that this break is much simpler. Gene sneaks into Finny's infirmary room, and Phineas accuses him of wanting to break something else in him. Gene flees, but returns to visit Phineas the next day. They talk about Finny's unsuccessful attempts to enlist. Gene observes that Phineas would have been lousy in the war: once bored, he would make friends with the enemy and get things "so scrambled up nobody would know who to fight any more." Finally they confront what happened in the tree. Gene agrees with Finny's analysis that "It was just some kind of blind impulse you had…. It wasn't anything you really felt against me, it wasn't some kind of hate you've felt all along. It wasn't anything personal." When Gene arrives at the infirmary the next day, he's told Phineas is dead: during the operation, some bone marrow escaped into his blood stream and stopped his heart. Dr. Stanpole likens the operating room to the war, where the risks "are just more formal than in other places."

Gene enlists in the Navy, but feels no sense of patriotism. He disagrees with Brinker's notion that the older generation is responsible for the war and with Finny's idea that the war is just a huge practical joke. Instead, he believes war is the result of "something ignorant in the human heart." He can't talk about Phineas because he can't accept the loss of his vitality, and he continues to feel guilty about his death. Gene realizes that he's ready for the war because he no longer feels any hatred. His war "ended before I ever put on a uniform; I was on active duty all my time at school; I killed my enemy there." He believes the real enemy is something he and the others have created out of their own fear.

Characters

Chet Douglass

Gene Forrester's rival for the position of class valedictorian. Unlike Gene, Chet has a genuine interest in learning and does not thrive simply on competition.

Finny

See Phineas

Gene Forrester

The narrator of A *Separate Peace*, Gene as an adult recalls himself at sixteen: a lonely intellectual with the tendency of analyzing his and everyone else's motives. At various times in the novel, he is highly competitive, selfish, insecure, and combative. On other occasions, he is courageous, mature, and dependable.

Throughout the novel, Gene compares and contrasts himself with his best friend, Finny, and often falls short in his own estimation. Although Gene is obviously the more scholarly of the two (Gene is academically near the top of his high school class, while Finny seldom achieves more than a "C" in his courses), Finny is the better athlete and more self-confident than his friend. Also troubling to Gene is that Finny openly flouts conventions but never gets punished for his acts. For example, on an occasion when Finny and Gene miss the mandatory school dinner, Finny cheerfully rambles a bizarre explanation to Mr. Prud'homme, the summer substitute teacher. Mr. Prud'homme, more amused than angry, decides not to punish the boys.

Gene observes many other occasions when Finny breaks the rules but never gets his comeuppance, because he has so much charm and self-confidence. He becomes increasingly jealous of Finny, and for a while he assumes Finny reciprocates those feelings. That Gene works systematically and diligently for his academic and athletic success and Finny's athletic achievements seem to come effortlessly to him fuels Gene's rivalry. Worse still for Gene, Finny doesn't even want acknowledgment for his accomplishments. For example, when Finny breaks the school swimming record with virtually no preparation, he insists that Gene—the only witness to the event—not tell anyone. For a while, it seems logical to Gene that Finny, as the school's best athlete, envies Gene his academic success. Ultimately, Finny proves Gene's theory wrong, when he genuinely encourages Gene to pursue his studies rather than join the "Super Suicide Society" one evening. Now Gene realizes that Finny never did envy him and finds this knowledge intolerable. In light of all the above, Gene impulsively jounces the limb Finny is standing on during a Super Suicide Society ritual, causing Finny his crippling accident.

As Ronald Weber writes in an article from *Studies in Short Fiction*, "It is Phineas's innocence that Gene cannot endure. As long as he can believe Phineas shares his enmity, he can find relief, but with this assurance gone, he stands condemned before himself and must strike out against his tormentor."

Ultimately, Gene matures through his introspection, coming to understand his terrible action against his friend. Shortly before Finny's death, he and Gene fully explore the dynamics of their relationship and the circumstances that caused Finny's accident. When Gene explains "it was just some ignorance inside me, some crazy thing inside me, something blind"—not a personal hatred of Finny or a premeditated action—Finny accepts the apology. As Ronald Weber has written, "Gene Forrester comes to learn that his war, the essential war, is fought on the battlefield within. Peace comes only when he faces up to the fact. The only escape, the price of peace, is self-awareness." James Ellis, in an *English Journal* article, puts it in similar terms: "Gene has discovered that his private evil, which caused him to hurt Phineas, is the same evil —only magnified—that results in war."

Mr. Hadley

Brinker Hadley's father, a World War I veteran whose patriotism offends both Brinker and Gene.

Brinker Hadley

Described as "the big name on campus," Brinker Hadley's characterization was actually based on the novelist Gore Vidal. In an interview with the *Exonion*, Knowles remembers Vidal as an "unusual and thriving" person, although he did not know him very well. In his realization of Hadley's slick temperament, Gene appreciates his own maturity. At one time, Gene would have ingratiated himself with someone like Hadley, but after Finny's fall Gene comes to prefer the sincerity of someone like Leper. Brinker Hadley also serves the function of being the character that arranges the mock tribunal to determine whether Gene is innocent or guilty in regard to Finny's fall.

Phil Latham

One of the less impressive authority figures at the Devon School, Phil Latham is the wrestling coach. His advice, "Give it the old college try," seems to pertain to all situations, whether they be sexual, psychological, or academic. He is not really an unsympathetic character, so much as a man without much intelligence or creativity.

Elwin Lepellier

A gentle, nonconformist student at Devon School, "Leper," as he is nicknamed, prefers snails and science projects to sports and competition. Ironically, he is the first student in the novel to enlist in the Army, because a deceptive recruiting film convinced Leper that Army life is a clean, pure experience. Soon after his induction into the Army, Leper realizes that he cannot adapt to the Spartan environment, and goes AWOL (absent without leave) in order to avoid being discharged as psychologically unfit for service. When Gene Forrester visits Leper in his Vermont home, the latter has been badly shaken by his Army experiences. Leper, aware of Gene's contempt for him, strikes back, calling him "a savage underneath." Leper also reveals that he knows Gene knocked Finny out of the tree earlier in the summer. Gene, realizing some truth to the "savage underneath" remark, physically strikes the frail Leper but does not hurt him badly.

While generally a pitiable character, Leper has a streak of pride. For example, at the tribunal scene, in which several Devon School students attempt to discover whether Gene really did cause Finny's traumatic fall, Leper will not reveal the extent of what he knows. Up until this point, most Devon School students have either ignored or ridiculed him, so he announces, "Why should I tell! Just because it happens to suit you!"

Leper

See Elwin Lepellier

Media Adaptations

- *A Separate Peace* was adapted as a film directed by Larry Peerce, starring John Heyl and Parker Stevenson, Paramount Pictures, 1972, available from Paramount Home Video, Home Vision Cinema. Although generally faithful to the novel, the film of the same name received mostly poor reviews. Typical was movie critic Leonard Maltin's opinion that the "story is morbid, acting incredibly amateurish, and direction has no feeling at all for the period."

Mr. Ludsbery

One of the permanent teachers at the Devon School, Mr. Ludsbery represents the worst stereotype of a schoolmaster: phony, a stickler for rules, and given to fatuous remarks such as "Has it been raining in your part of town?" When he reproaches Gene for "[slipping] in any number of ways since last year," Gene is reminded of his friend Finny and does not care about anything else the teacher says.

Mr. Patch-Withers

A stern history teacher at the Devon School, he and his wife give a tea party for the students. There, he shows a gender side by not punishing Finny for flagrantly violating the dress code.

Mrs. Patch-Withers

The wife of the history teacher at the Devon School, she is appalled to see Finny wear his official school tie as a belt to her party.

Phineas

One of the two central characters in the novel. Phineas, also known as Finny, is Devon School's best athlete and a handsome, self-confident teenager. Despite or because of these qualities, he is also arguably the most innocent of all the characters in *A Separate Peace.* For example, just before he and Gene fall asleep on the beach one night, Finny honestly declares that Gene is his "best pal."

Somewhat taken aback, Gene cannot return the compliment and reflects "It was a courageous thing to say. Exposing a sincere emotion nakedly like that at the Devon School was the next thing to suicide." Finny is naive in other ways as well. When Gene complains about not having enough time to study, Finny is genuinely puzzled. "I didn't know you needed to study," he said simply. "I didn't think you ever did. I thought it came to you." Since Finny excels at sports with a minimum of effort—Gene witnesses his breaking the school swimming record with no preparation—he does not understand that Gene works diligently to be at the top of his class scholastically.

In Hallman Bell Bryant's *A Separate Peace: The War Within*, the author compares Finny to many literary or historical figures. For example, he brings to mind Mark Twain's Huckleberry Finn; just as Huck could not accept the Old Testament story of Moses because he did not have any "stock" in dead folks, Finny doubts the authenticity of the Latin language because it is a "dead language." Many critics have compared Finny to J. D. Salinger's Holden Caulfield in *Catcher in the Rye* for both characters' unpretentiousness, honesty, and anti-establishment attitudes. However, other critics dissent; for example, Granville Hicks wrote in a *Saturday Review* article that Finny's spontaneity and unconventionality were not, like Holden's, a form of protest against authority; they were an inherent part of his nature. At one point in *A Separate Peace*, Gene compares the sleeping Finny to Lazarus.

After Gene causes Finny his crippling fall, Finny loses some of his innocence. Ironically, however, because of his physical disability, he becomes increasingly dependent on Gene; in fact, he even comes to see Gene as an "extension of himself," while always suspecting that Gene caused his accident. Dr. Stanpole medically explains Finny's unexpected death in these terms: "As I was moving the bone some of the marrow must have ... gone directly to his heart and stopped it." Symbolically, of course, Finny's death can be interpreted otherwise; although he forgave Gene on some level, Finny's heartbreak still lingered.

Given the distance of time and the impact of maturity, the adult Gene realizes Finny's principal virtue is his lack of malice. As James Ellis puts it, "Because of his ability to admit only as much of the ugliness of life as he could assimilate, Phineas was unique."

Mr. Prud'homme

A substitute teacher at the Devon School for the summer. Given that he is not entirely familiar with the rules, he is not so strict in enforcing them.

Cliff Quackenbush

The opposite of Finny in nearly every respect, he is also Gene's nemesis. The crew manager at the Devon School, Quackenbush is a colorless, humorless character, someone who never seems to have been a child emotionally. Openly scornful of Gene for becoming assistant crew manager, Quackenbush calls him to his face "a maimed son-of-a-bitch," and a fight between them ensues. Although Quackenbush never realizes it, the insult heightens Gene's guilt and confusion over causing Finny's accident. He also touches a nerve when he sarcastically asks Gene "Who the hell are you anyway?" because introverted Gene often seems uncertain as to why he acts as he does.

Dr. Stanpole

One of the more sympathetic adults in the novel, Dr. Stanpole is a well-meaning character who speaks with a vocabulary too sophisticated for the students at Devon School. To what extent his skill as a doctor is responsible for Finny's death remains uncertain.

Themes

Guilt and Innocence

In John Knowles's novel that chronicles the coming of age of two prep-school friends, one character—Finny—loses much of his trustfulness and innocence, while the other—Gene—progresses toward self-knowledge and maturity. That *A Separate Peace* takes place in the first half of the 1940s explains so many references to war. In this novel, however, the real struggle is fought in the hearts of the characters, not on the battlefield. After Gene causes Finny's crippling fall, everything that follows, as Knowles has written, is "one long abject confession, a *mea culpa*, a tale of crime—if a crime has been committed—and of no punishment. It is a story of growth through tragedy." While Gene does eventually reconcile to his transgression against Finny, the process takes many years. Gene obtains some peace of mind through his final encounter with Finny, in which he shows both humility and understanding of Finny's pacifist nature. But it is only as a thirty-something adult revisiting his former school that Gene has accumulated the wisdom and maturity to fully understand the significance of what happened in his adolescence. In reconciling with his guilty conscience, Gene does more than understand the dark side of human nature. He also absorbs the best of Finny's code of behavior, "a way of sizing up the world with erratic and entirely personal reservations." While Gene will never again possess the innocence he recalls from the summer of 1942, as James M. Mellard writes in *Studies in Short Fiction*, "if he and the others fall short of Finny's standard, as they must, they will still gain from having reached for it."

Finny's development in the latter half of the novel can be seen in terms of loss of innocence. Since he is now physically incapacitated, unlikely to ever regain his athletic powers, his carefree ways are also gone. Although he superficially denies the existence of World War II, he secretly goes to great lengths to enlist. However, since no army will accept him due to his accident, Finny loses much of his self-confidence. He increasingly lives vicariously through Gene, coming to perceive Gene as "an extension of himself," but he always knows on some level that Gene deliberately caused his accident. Although Dr. Stanpole gives a medical explanation for Finny's death, the event can also be seen symbolically. As Douglas Alley in an *English Journal* article writes of Finny, "For him, there could be no growing up. A loss of innocence could only result in death."

War

On one level, *A Separate Peace* can be read as a war novel. Its title is taken from Ernest Hemingway's novel *A Farewell to Arms*, in which the book's protagonist, Lt. Frederic Henry, declares his own private armistice during World War I.

However, unlike Hemingway's novel, Knowles's book does not concern soldiers on the battlefield; rather, it focuses on the impact of war on the lives of male adolescents, none of whom have yet engaged in combat. Despite their lack of direct involvement in World War II, boys who were not quite of draft age were often preoccupied by the American war effort. The idea of avoiding military service in World War II was unthinkable to most young men; the questions were when they would be called to serve and which branch of the military would accept them. As Gene Forrester in the late 1950s reflects on the impact of World War II for him, "The war was and is reality for me. I still instinctively live and think in its atmosphere."

Topics for Further Study

- Explore the reasons for the American involvement in World War II. Compare the American degree of popular support to that of such other wars as World War I, the Vietnam War, and the Korean War.

- Compare and contrast three significant fictional works about World War II. Some possibilities include James Jones's novel *From Here to Eternity*, Norman Mailer's novel *The Naked and the Dead*, and Arthur Miller's play *All My Sons*.

- Discuss the economic impact of World War II on the United States and on Europe.

As Gene recalls, the American war effort had enormous domestic implications on his generation. For example, since nearly all of the Devon School's younger faculty were away serving in the military or in war-related jobs, substitute teachers—usually men between the ages of fifty and seventy—were brought into the school. Given the great age differences between the students and their new teachers, the former did not usually see the latter as accessible role models. Hence, the bonds between the students intensified. Yet, the new faculty members were not unkind; as Gene recalls, "I think we reminded them of what peace was like, we boys of sixteen. We registered with no draft board, we had taken no physical examinations…. We were carefree and wild, and I suppose we could be thought of as a sign of the life the war was being fought to preserve. Anyway, they were more indulgent toward us than at any other time."

The American war effort impacted everyday life in more general ways. For example, as Gene recalls, "Nylon, meat, gasoline, and steel are rare. There are too many jobs and not enough workers. Money is very easy to earn but rather hard to spend, because there isn't very much to buy."

Style

Point of View

Told in first person ("I") by Gene Forrester, a man in his thirties recalling his adolescence, A *Separate Peace* begins with Gene's visit to the Devon School. The first pages of the novel mainly describe the physical landscape of the institution; the rest tells Gene's story, a tale in which he serves as both an observer and a participant at the center of the action. As Ronald Weber notes, "Generally, first-person narration gives the reader a heightened sense of immediacy, a sense of close involvement with the life of the novel.... With Knowles' s novel, however, this is not the case ... throughout it he remains somewhat outside the action and detached from the narrator, observing the life of the novel rather than submerged in it." This is not intended as a criticism, however. As Weber explains, Knowles's choice of narration is "a highly-calculated effect.... It indicates a sharply different thematic intention, and one that is rooted in a skillful alteration of the conventional method of first-person telling."

It is important to remember that Gene, through the distance of time—specifically fifteen years—has arrived at a level of self-knowledge that few teenagers could achieve. Had Knowles limited the perspective to the highly introspective, but still adolescent Gene, *A Separate Peace* would have been told in a very different tone. As Ronald Weber writes, "Gene's voice ... is dispassionate, reflective, and controlled; it is, in his own words, a voice from which fury is gone, dried up at its source long before the telling begins."

Setting

Most of the action of the novel is confined to the Devon School, the prep school based on Phillips Exeter. An exception is found in Chapter 10, in which Gene visits his friend Leper in his family's Vermont home. When Gene revisits the Devon School, he is particularly interested in confronting two fearful places on campus. The first is the First Academy Building, a Georgian-style red-brick structure, in which a group of Devon students brought Gene to accuse him of causing the accident that crippled Finny's life. On the stairs of the First Academy Building, another misfortune occurred which ultimately ended Finny's life. The second place of significance is the tree from which Gene and Finny leaped in their "Super Suicide Society" escapades. While the adult Gene recalls the tree as an enormous, forbidding structure, when he actually rediscovers it, the tree appears much smaller and similar to all the other trees in the vicinity.

In terms of time, A *Separate Peace* skips back and forth between the early 1940s and the late 1950s. Again, this time difference creates a retrospective which allows the narrator Gene to relate the events with more depth and analysis.

Symbolism

A Separate Peace is a book full of symbolism. One pair of symbols can be found in two rivers that flow through the school: the Devon and the Naguamsett. Gene remembers the freshwater Devon River fondly, for this was the body of water that he and Finny had leaped into many times from the tree. Ironically, after Finny's accident, Gene does not remember the Devon River with fear or disgust; the river to him symbolizes the carefree summer days, a peaceful time. On the other hand, the Naguamsett River ("governed by imaginable factors like the Gulf Stream, the Polar Ice Cap, and the moon") is an ugly, marshy, saline river into which Gene falls after a fight with quarrelsome Cliff Quackenbush. If the Devon River represents serenity, Gene associates the Naguamsett with war and winter.

Another obvious pair of symbols is in the contrast between the war being fought abroad and the relative tranquility of the Devon School, particularly in its summer session. To Gene "the war was and is reality," yet by completing his final year at the Devon School he is literally avoiding military service. Still, he and his classmates realize it is only a matter of time before they enlist or are drafted. So, if the war represents a harsh reality that schoolboys like Gene must eventually confront, then Gene and Finny's "gypsy" summer spent at the Devon School denotes illusion. In the only summer session in the school's long history, the students defy many rules, still maintain the faculty's goodwill, create new games such as "Blitzball," and begin unheard-of clubs such as the "Super Suicide Society of the Summer Session." The summer is a period of escape for Devon School's students. As Gene observes, "Bombs in Central Europe were completely unreal to us here, not because we couldn't imagine it ... but because our place here was too fair for us to accept something like that." Still, Gene realizes that the "gypsy" summer spirit will not last indefinitely; "official class leaders and politicians" will replace the "idiosyncratic, leaderless band" of the summer. To recapture the carefree summer spirit, Gene and Finny have a "Winter Carnival" in which "there was going to be no government," and "on this day even the schoolboy egotism of Devon was conjured away."

Epiphany

An epiphany is a sudden flash of perception into the nature of a thing or event. In his most provocative insight into human nature, Gene realizes toward the conclusion of *A Separate Peace* "that wars were not made by generations and their special stupidities, but that wars were made instead by something ignorant in the human heart." As James Ellis writes, "Gene has discovered that his private evil, which caused him to hurt Phineas, is the same evil—only magnified—that results in war."

American Feelings about War

Although first published in 1959 in England, *A Separate Peace* is about an earlier period, specifically the early 1940s when United States had declared its involvement in World War II. It must be remembered that World War II brought out enormous patriotism in most Americans, whether they were actually working in war-related jobs, engaged in combat, or neither. While intelligent adolescents such as Gene Forrester and Hadley Brinker in *A Separate Peace* might have mixed feelings about being drafted or enlisting in the war, shirking responsibility (in other words, draft dodging) was virtually unthinkable. Elwin "Leper" Lepellier, a major character in Knowles's novel, enlists in the war and does go AWOL (absent without leave). However, although he is often a sincere, sympathetic character, he does not ultimately emerge a hero.

It is also worth remembering that when *A Separate Peace* was first published in the United States in 1960, the Korean War had been over for about seven years, and American involvement in the War in Vietnam had not yet escalated to horrific proportions. There was little protest over compulsory enrollment in the military—the draft— or the U.S.'s role in Vietnam in the early 1960s. As

U.S. involvement and troop movement escalated after 1965, however, public support for the war dimninished and many young antiwar protesters responded by burning their draft notices. Thus, while numerous critics submitted scholarly articles on Knowles's novel throughout the 1960s, by the end of the decade, the book was being considered in light of the devastation that the Vietnam War had wrought. Interestingly, left-wing and conservative critics praised *A Separate Peace* in different ways. The former found its antiwar sentiments appropriate and timely, particularly in light of what they perceived as the threat of atomic warfare. Yet right-wing reviewers also liked the book, often commending its treatment of original sin and redemption.

Compare & Contrast

- **1940s:** In the middle of World War II, the United States had compulsory draft registration for young men, most of whom expected to eventually enlist in the military.

  Early 1960s: While the United States still had compulsory draft registration for young men, only a few were being called up for military duty in Vietnam.

  Today: Reinstated in the early 1980s after a brief dismissal in the 1970s, draft registration is still required for young men in America, although there is little chance of being called up into a military that is currently all-volunteer.

- **1940s:** America declared its involvement in World War II, and had troops in Europe and the Pacific.
  Early 1960s: Although America had sent some troops to Vietnam, their commitment to the war effort was insignificant at the time compared to the escalation after 1965.
  Today: The United States of America is not involved in any major war effort, and relies on all-volunteer armed forces.

- **1940s:** The path to success for young men from upper-class white families often led from the best prep school to an Ivy League university.
  Early 1960s: University enrollment soared as the baby boom generation reached college age. Many government programs existed to help more young people from middle-class and impoverished backgrounds attain a college education.
  Today: College graduates still have higher average salaries than people with less education. With government financing for higher

education on the decline, universities find themselves competing for the enrollment dollars of a decreasing college-age population.

Education and Adolescence in the 1960s

Many of the young people of the 1960s grew up in a different atmosphere from the youth of the 1990s. After the Soviet launch of the Sputnik satellite in 1957, education was beginning to be emphasized as important not only to individual success but to the success of the nation. Not only were new teaching methods and standards being put into place, but the federal government began taking a greater role in funding and setting policy for education. College enrollment soared, as young people saw higher education as providing a chance to get ahead in life. Nevertheless, there were many problems with the educational system. Segregation persisted in many areas and opportunities were limited for women. The all-white, male prep school of *A Separate Peace* was still thriving in 1960. It was seen as a student's best chance to get into the best private universities, so pressure to succeed could be great.

The culture of the young also came of age in the 1960s. When the first American edition of the novel appeared in 1960, the United States had its youngest elected president, John F. Kennedy, who at the age of forty-three had defeated Vice President Richard M. Nixon by a margin of only 113,000 votes out of more than 69 million cast. The children of the "Baby Boom"—the large population surge that began after World War 11—were adolescents. As the decade progressed and the Baby Boomers reached college, they became an increasingly vocal part of American politics and culture. Brought up in prosperity and peace, these children questioned the morality and authority of their parents' generation and pursued individual fulfillment. Their search for meaning and identity is reflected in Gene's narrative of his own adolescent years.

Critical Overview

John Knowles's *A Separate Peace*, a critical success from its first printing, has evolved into one of the most frequently read novels in American high schools today. In fact, in the words of its author, it has captured a "destiny apart" from his own. Although Knowles has published many other novels, essays, and works of nonfiction, none has received the critical attention or praise of *A Separate Peace*. While that novel no longer commands the massive scholarly attention that it did throughout the 1960s, according to Hallman Bell Bryant, it has gone through at least seventy printings and earns Knowles somewhere between $30,000 and $40,000 a year in royalties.

Right from the start, *A Separate Peace* received extremely favorable notices. Since it was first published by Secker and Warburg in London, England, the British reviewers were the first to write what they liked about the book. The most significant of these pieces appeared in the *Times Literary Supplement* section on 1 May 1959. This review congratulated Knowles for having written a "novel of altogether exceptional power and distinction." Other English critics praised *A Separate Peace*, many of them saying it was the best American novel since J. D. Salinger's *Catcher in the Rye*, which had been published in 1953. In her *Manchester Guardian* review, Ann Duchene enjoyed the "tenderness and restraint" that Knowles expressed for his two major characters, Gene and Finny.

After the favorable English reception, the publishing firm of Macmillan bought the rights to the novel and issued the first American edition in February, 1960. Among the earliest reviews, Edmund Fuller wrote in the *New York Times* that Knowles was a writer "already skilled in craft and discerning in his perceptions." He went on to say the World War II background was more central to the action of the novel than the Devon School setting, which he realized was based on Exeter. Although Fuller found several incidents in the book to be unconvincing, he thought the novel's "major truths" more than compensated for this shortcoming. Among the few negative reviews of *A Separate Peace*, a *Commonweal* critic shrugged it off as "one more foray into the territory of guilt earned in adolescence." While most other American critics found the book a compelling achievement, several reserved criticism for the trial scene in which several Devon students attempt to ascertain the extent of Gene Forrester's involvement in Finny's accident. Fifteen years later, after *A Separate Peace* had been made into a movie of the same name, Linda Heinz of *Literature Film Quarterly* wrote that she found the mock tribunal in both the book and the movie unconvincing.

Despite *A Separate Peace's* immediate critical acclaim, it did not become a best-seller, nor did any book clubs immediately select it for inclusion. However, its sales picked up considerably after it won the William Faulkner Foundation Award, as well as the Richard and Hinda Rosenthal Foundation Award. John K. Crabbe, writing for the *English Journal* in 1963, recommended high school teachers of American literature consider Knowles's novel as an alternative to J. D. Salinger's popular *Catcher in the Rye*. Many teachers were relieved to do so, having had some apprehensions about the profanity in *Catcher*. James Ellis, also writing for the *English Journal*, called William Golding's *Lord of the Flies* and *A Separate Peace* major finds for the high school classroom. By the middle 1960s, many English teachers had made *A Separate Peace* a part of their curriculum.

By the early 1970s, the barrage of articles analyzing the novel had subsided. However, even in the late 1970s—almost twenty years after the book had been published—some critique and analysis persisted. For example, in George-Michael Sarotte's book *Like a Brother, Like a Lover*, published in 1978, the author speculates that Gene may have homoerotic feelings for Finny. As late as 1992, the *English Journal* was still extolling the virtues of *A Separate Peace* in the article "Still Good Reading: Adolescent Novels Written Before 1967."

Sources

Douglas Alley, "Teaching Emerson Through 'A Separate Peace,'" in *English Journal*, January, 1981, pp. 19-23.

Hallman Bell Bryant, *"A Separate Peace": The War Within*, Twayne, 1990.

John K. Crabbe, "On the Playing Fields of Devon," in *English Journal*, Vol. 58, 1969, pp. 519-20.

Anne Duchene, in a review of *A Separate Peace* in *Manchester Guardian*, May 1, 1959.

James Ellis, "'A Separate Peace': A Fall From Innocence," in *English Journal*, May, 1964, pp. 313-18.

Edmund Fuller, "Shadow of Mars," in *New York Times Book Review*, February 7, 1960.

Linda Heinz, "'A Separate Peace': Filming the War Within," in *Literature Film Quarterly*, No. 3, 1975, p. 168.

John Knowles, "The Young Writer's Real Friends," *The Writer*, Vol. 75, July, 1962, pp. 12-14.

John Knowles, "My Separate Peace," in *Esquire*, March, 1985, pp. 106–9.

James M. Mellard, "Counterpoint and 'Double Vision' in 'A Separate Peace'," in *Studies in Short Fiction*, No. 4,1966, pp. 127-35.

J. Noffsinger, A. M. Rice, *et al.* "Still Good

Reading: Adolescent Novels Written Before 1967,"
English Journal, April, 1992, p. 7.

A review of *A Separate Peace*, in *Commonweal*,
December 9, 1960.

A review of *A Separate Peace*, in *Times Literary
Supplement*, May 1, 1959.

Ronald Weber, "Narrative Method in 'A Separate
Peace'," in *Studies in Short Fiction 3*, 1965, pp. 63-
72.

For Further Study

Hallman Bell Bryant, "Symbolic Names in Knowles's *A Separate Peace,"* in *Names*, Vol. 34, No. 1, March, 1986, pp. 83-8.

> An analysis of some of the character's names in the novel.

Concise Dictionary of Literary Biography Broadening Views, 1968-1988, Gale, 1989, pp. 120-35.

> Biographical information on John Knowles and his work. Includes revised typescript from one of Knowles's works.

Jay L. Halio, "John Knowles's Short Novels," *Studies in Short Fiction* Vol. I, Winter, 1964, pp. 107-09.

> A survey of several of Knowles's shorter novels.

Granville Hicks, "The Good Have a Quiet Heroism," in *Saturday Review*, March 5, 1960, p. 15.

> Early review which praises *A Separate Peace*, and analyzes Finny's character, concluding he is not really a hero.

Isabel Quigly, *The Heirs of Tom Brown: The English School Story*, Oxford University Press,

1984.

>This book-length study looks at the genre of the "school story" and is useful in an analysis of Knowles's novel as it fits into this genre.

Michael-George Sarotte, *Like a Brother, Like a Lover*, Doubleday, 1978.

>In this book-length study of male homosexuality in literature, Sarotte argues that Gene's suppressed homoerotic emotions for Finny are integral to his character.